"This book is dedicated to all the Mom's who scarified their dreams for their kids."

Michella G

Table of Contents

Introduction 6

Chapter 1 - Understanding the Mompreneurial Mindset................. 9
   The Spirit of an Entrepreneur.. 10
   How to Nurture Your Entrepreneurial Spirit.. 12

Chapter 2 – 7 Common Traits of an Mompreneur......................... 17

Chapter 3 – What is Grit?.. 24
   Characteristics of Grit.. 25

Chapter 4 – Why You Need to Develop Grit to Become Successful ... 30
   It is Important for Survival 31
   It Helps You Emerge Victoriously... 31
   It Enables You to Pursue Your Dreams 31
   Grit Makes You Successful 32
   Grit Improves Your Self-Control 32
   Grit Makes Your Fearless 33
   It Unleashes Your Optimism, Confidence, and Creative Power.............. 34

Chapter 5 – Habits of Gritty People.. 35
   Always Show You're in Complete Control... 36
   Learn Lessons from Your Past... 37
   Don't Stress Over Things You Can't Control 38
   Never Criticize or Complain 38
   Be Conscious of Your Blessings 39

Celebrate the Success of Those Around You 40
Focus on Impressing Yourself 40
Be Specific 41
Act on Your Objective 42
Face Your Fears 42

Chapter 6 – How To Find Your Passion 44

Chapter 7 – Face Your Fears 50

Chapter 8 – Build Your Perseverance 55
How to Deal with Unexpected Issues 60

Chapter 9 - Become More Resilient and Boost Your Stubbornness ... 64
Why Stubbornness is an Important Part of Grit 67

Chapter 10 – Boost Your Confidence, Optimism, and Creativity 70
Tips for Boosting Your Self-Confidence 71
Tips for Boosting Your Positive Thinking 74
Tips for Tapping into Your Creative Side 76

Conclusion 78

Introduction

Every year in the United States, more than 627,000 new businesses open, according to estimates from the Small Business Administration, SBA. That's more than half a million people deciding to leave their 9 to 5 job and set out on their own. Unfortunately, not everyone is cut out to be a small business owner, as evident by the nearly 595,000 businesses that close every year. To those companies that are able to get off the ground and running, only 51 percent are able to remain in business for more than five years.

With such disheartening numbers, you may be wondering if you should venture out on your own and start a business, and whether or not you'll succeed as an entrepreneur. The good news is, anyone can become a successful entrepreneur with the right mindset. The mindset of successful entrepreneurs is different from everyone else. There are many ways in which they think and act differently. When you know what you are looking for, you can begin to think and act like a successful entrepreneur.

When it comes to creating a successful business, like any journey, you need to have a map. Having a plan of where you need to go will help you get to your destination in the fastest time possible. This book is meant to be your map and help you become a successful entrepreneur, as fast as possible. To be truly successful, in anything that you do, you have to have the right mindset. This is true whether you are an elite athlete, a world champion, or a billionaire business owner. All of these people share a specific mindset, and if you want to be a successful entrepreneur and be successful in life, you will need to develop this same, robust and focused mindset.

The more important question that you will have to ask yourself at the beginning of your journey to entrepreneurial success is why are you doing this? The answer that you give is one that will have to last you for the majority of your life, so the answer better be good. It has to be good enough that you won't falter, even at the worst of times.

Staying focused and driven to reach your goals and find success will require you to rewire your brain. However, if you've never reached a low point or a turning point, how are you going to do this? How can you get into the zone and stay there, all the time, no matter what? Finding the zone and staying there month after month, year after year isn't an easy task. That's why the question of why you're doing this is so important.

Chapter 1 – Understanding the Mompreneur Mindset

Who you are, what you think, your personal habits, your attitude, your thoughts and your beliefs will determine the results you get, regardless of what you do in your life. Developing an entrepreneurial mindset is one of the best things you can do. It helps you to challenge yourself to recognize, overcome, and change what isn't working in your life.

As a business owner, you have to quickly come to the understanding that your mindset is your business. It represents the path you'll take and how quickly you'll achieve success. The entrepreneur's mindset begins with your excitement about the success that is still to come. Successful entrepreneurs can see the opportunity put before them and spends hours daydreaming about the success they will achieve and how it will feel when it becomes a reality. It's what fuels the fire. Without it, the motivation for any entrepreneurial venture will quickly fade.

Many people believe that a successful business relies solely on the business model. However, there is more to it than this. To truly find success as an entrepreneur, you have to develop an entrepreneurial mindset. So, what does having an entrepreneurial mindset entail?

The Spirit of an Entrepreneur

When you envision what an entrepreneur is, you probably think of a hard-working individual, who is smart and knows how to network. Someone that is creative and is able to take calculated risks. They might have outstanding leadership skills and other qualities that make them successful. While these qualities are integral parts of every entrepreneur, not all successful entrepreneurs have these qualities in abundance. The fact of the matter is that some entrepreneurs will lack some qualities altogether while having a wealth of others. So, what is the commonality between all entrepreneurs; what is the one thing that all entrepreneurs possess?

For 99 percent of successful entrepreneurs, they have the spirit of entrepreneurship in common. This means they are unable to accept the status quo. Deep down, successful entrepreneurs are rebels. They are rebels who are unwilling to conform to standards set by others. They push themselves past these set boundaries. It is this spirit that allows them to face a plethora of problems and see the solutions and opportunities presented. It is the same spirit that allows them to rise above the fear of failure and overcome doubts. It allows them to improvise, innovate, invent, and create new paths and businesses, where none exist. The entrepreneurial spirit is the undying belief in one's own ability. It is the resolute belief that we all have a role to play in shaping society through the creation of business solutions for some of life's most common problems.

Most of the qualities that entrepreneurs possess are a manifestation of the entrepreneurial spirit. When faced with a problem, entrepreneurs will exercise resourcefulness. When faced with a situation that they can't immediately control, a successful entrepreneur will always persevere.

As a budding entrepreneur, one thing that you must understand is that the entrepreneurial spirit transcends business.

How to Nurture Your Entrepreneurial Spirit

If you are continually looking at the world around you and seeing it the way you want it to be rather than how it is, this is your entrepreneurial spirit waiting to be unleashed. This is because at the core of the entrepreneurial spirit is the ability to wonder what's possible.

The entrepreneurial spirit can be boiled down to the six P's: Passion, Path, Positivity, People, Perseverance, and Productivity. These are the quintessential tools that will make it possible for you to reach your goals and find entrepreneurial success.

Passion

Passion is the fire that drives you. It is why you want to become an entrepreneur. It is what gives you the motivation to engage in whatever venture you wish to participate in. It is the need that you have to make a difference in the world around you.

As you set out on your entrepreneurial journey, you need to take the time to figure out what you are genuinely passionate about. When you tie your passion to a business idea, it will help to fuel your drive to succeed. Without passion, you will never find real entrepreneurial success or freedom. In fact, if you start a business that you aren't passionate about, you are no better than the person staying at a job they hate.

The idea behind every successful business is the need to solve a problem. By tying your passion to that problem, you will set yourself up for entrepreneurial success.

Path

While it is your passion that motivates you to work on your business, a path provides you the map for actualizing your business idea to ensure that when you run into challenges and experience setbacks, you will persevere. When you have a path to follow, you will be able to obtain the success that you desire, because it allows you to take impactful action and be productive.

Business success doesn't come easy. When you have a roadmap, taking action is more natural, which results in being able to achieve business success easily. Your path should detail all the things that you need to do to achieve business success.

Positivity

Positivity touches and influences everything we do in business, as well as life. If you establish a company and expect and anticipate it to fail, you've ultimately created a self-fulfilling prophecy, because you attract what you manifest through your thoughts. If the views about your business are negative, you will see negative growth as a result.

Practicing the power of positivity, especially when you face challenges and setbacks, will permeate every aspect of your business. Your positive thoughts will help you to find innovative solutions to even the most demanding problems.

People

To be a successful entrepreneur, you have to look for and build strong networks. Your success as an entrepreneur hinges on your ability to connect and interact with people. This includes suppliers, employees, business colleagues, mentors, and other people around you. Without a support system, your passion for your business will falter, along with your motivation to implement the steps on your path. Your support system will help keep you motivated, cheer you on during difficult times, hold you accountable, and mentor you. This will help make your journey to entrepreneurial success all worthwhile.

Throughout your entrepreneurial journey, you need to build a robust support system that consists of more than your employees and immediate family. You need to learn how to become a proficient networker and understand the importance of attending social networking events. Networking like a pro takes a ton of practice, but with enough time you can become a networking star and build a strong group of connections for your business success.

Perseverance

Entrepreneurs who are successful, got that way because they have never given up on their dreams. The very nature of an entrepreneur is not complementary to the spirit of giving up or giving in. If you lack the ability to stare hardships in the face and shrug off challenges you encounter, you will never achieve business success because hard work and perseverance are what it takes to be successful.

Your business success hinges on your ability to look failure in the face and find the courage to trudge forward until you've accomplished your goals. This requires you to increase your grit and perseverance.

Productivity

The one thing that will determine how fast or slowly you achieve business success is your ability to use time well. If rather than working on the steps outlined in your path, you aimlessly surf your social media networks, watch videos on YouTube, or spend your day surfing the web, it will take you years to achieve success as an entrepreneur.

Achieving success as an entrepreneur takes a lot of hard work. The hard work that you do has to be laser-focused because if you lack focus, achieving success will take longer. You have to focus on completing one task at a time, along with minimizing distractions and procrastination.

When you foster these six tools, you will begin to see business opportunities everywhere around you and be able to capitalize on these opportunities because you will be in the right mindset.

Chapter 2 – 7 Common Traits of an Mompreneur

Not everyone is cut out to be an entrepreneur. There are specific traits that you have to have in order to find success as an entrepreneur. To see the results that you are looking for in your entrepreneurial journey, you have to begin to develop some of the same characteristics that are commonly found in successful entrepreneurs.

Successful people have certain habits and ways of conducting themselves. This provides them with the ability to accomplish more during the day and allows them to have the right mindset. While some people are born with these characteristics, most people who dream of becoming successful entrepreneurs have to work to develop these traits and incorporate them into their daily lives. Here are the seven characteristics that you need to possess if you want to find success as an entrepreneur.

Tenacity

The first characteristic that most successful entrepreneurs possess is tenacity. When it comes to business, tenacity means that you don't take failure personally and you keep working, sometimes for years, to get the things you want in your life. A tenacious entrepreneur will never give up and can bounce back when they face setbacks and run into challenges. When they run into roadblocks and experience setbacks, they don't give up; instead the try something new or try doing it another way.

Other people tend to give up and quit when they become frustrated or when something is too hard. Entrepreneurs, on the other hand, merely shrug their shoulders and move forward with their plan. It is often wrongly assumed that successful people don't experience failure. However, they have a higher instance of experiencing failures in their lives because they never give up trying. The difference between successful people and the rest of the population is that people who are successful understand that failure is just a part of the game and continue moving forward in the face of failure.

Passion

It is a common assumption that successful entrepreneurs are driven by money. However, most entrepreneurs will tell you that they are driven by their passion for their service or product. They are driven by their need to solve a problem and make life better, more comfortable, and cheaper. They believe that they will be able to change the world. They are excited by what they are doing and believe that their passion will get them through the difficult times.

Having a passion that is based on your business' specific mission provides an intrinsic drive and belief that the internal reward will help sustain you between paydays. It is your passion for what you do that will push you to go the extra mile. Your passion will provide you with the excitement to go to work every day and get things done. You'll begin to be excited to see what can happen.

Tolerance of Ambiguity

This personality trait is defined merely by the ability to withstand the fear of uncertainty and potential failure. Successful entrepreneurs are inherent risk-takers. The ability to control one's anxiety is the most critical characteristic of successful entrepreneurs. Entrepreneurs face an abundance of fears; the fear of humiliation, the fear of running out of cash, the fear of missing payroll, the fear of having to declare bankruptcy, the list goes on. The successful entrepreneur is able to look fear in the face and push forward with their plan.

The ultimate entrepreneurial test happens on the mental battlefield. You have to decide to either go with the fear and quit or push through the fear and move forward in pursuing your goals. Successful entrepreneurs always push through the fear. They are able to control their thoughts and mentally commit to their plan and the actions that follow. The entrepreneur will look at a situation and know that they have some control over the outcome.

Vision

One of the defining traits of all successful entrepreneurs is their ability to spot an opportunity and imagine something where others haven't. Entrepreneurs have an inherent curiosity about the world around them that provides them with the ability to identify overlooked niches and put them at the forefront of innovation and emerging fields. They are able to imagine another world and have the ability to communicate their vision to others.

Successful entrepreneurs are always looking for ways to the change things around them and make them different, unique and better. They are willing to take the risk to see their vision become a reality because they know that it is going to be something big.

Self-Confidence

A critical entrepreneurial trait is self-confidence. If you don't believe that you have what it takes to do something, then chances are you won't succeed in your business venture. You have to have faith in your thoughts and opinions and know that you are capable of accomplishing anything that you put your mind to achieving. You have to be sure that your product or service is something that the world needs and that you can deliver it to overcome the naysayers in your life.

Researchers describe this as task-specific confidence. It's a belief that turns the risk proposition around and provides you with the assurance that you can get the job done based on the research you've conducted. You have to have the confidence and be willing to take calculated risks. Successful entrepreneurs know that they are right and are confident that they are making the right decisions for their life.

Flexibility

Your ability to survive in business depends on your ability to adapt and be flexible to the continually changing world. The final product or service that you offer will likely look different from when you started. Flexibility is what allows you to respond to the changing tastes and market conditions and is essential if you want to be a successful entrepreneur.

If you are unable to remain flexible in your journey to entrepreneurial success, you are going to be in for a huge disappointment. This is because in business something will eventually go wrong. Those who are successful understand that things aren't always going to go the way that they want or plan. They are able to see when things are going off track, figure out why they are going off track, and make the necessary adjustments to get back on the path.

Time-Management

The difference between successful people and the rest of the population is that they are able to properly manage the time that they have. They are highly organized individuals, which allows them to complete tasks without wasting time. This results in them being able to accomplish more throughout the day, without having to put in excessive hours.

Developing these characteristics and incorporating them into your daily life can make your entrepreneurial venture much more manageable and can help you reach the success you've always dreamed of possessing. Take some time to look at your life and see which of these characteristics you already possess and which ones you need to develop.

Chapter 3 – What is Grit?

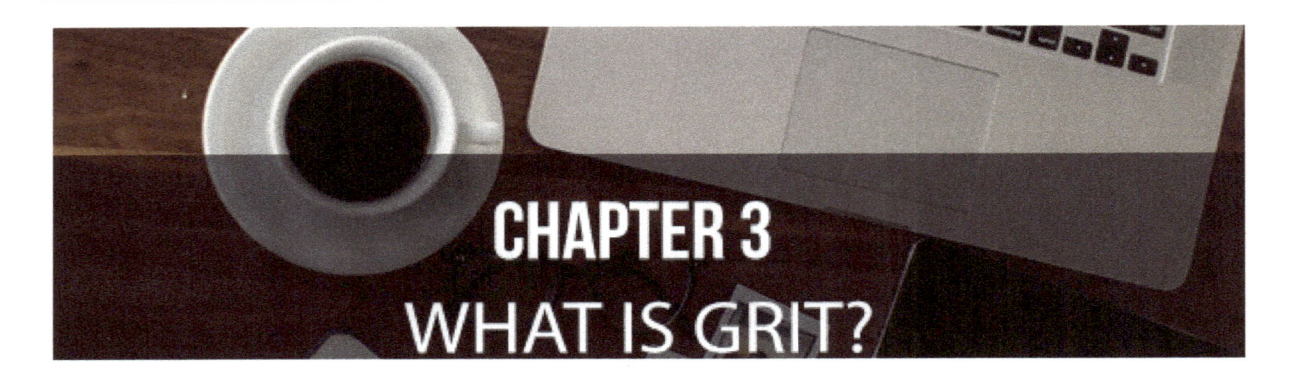

Grit is the unique quality that makes you willing and ready to commit yourself to your long-term goals and pursue them despite any adversity that you may face. It is defined as having a firm character and an indomitable spirit. This means that gritty people have a resolute attitude and stay firm on the decisions they make.

Renowned American psychologist, Angela Duckworth, has thoroughly researched the subject and made many discoveries on grit. She states that if you have grit, you have the passion for the goals that you pursue and have the perseverance to go after it in spite of the challenges and setbacks that you might experience.

She also discovered that those people who lack grit fail to reach and fulfill their potential, even when they are incredibly talented.

While the exact essence of grit is still elusive, there are some significant characteristics of grit that you have to possess in order to be genuinely determined and tenacious and find entrepreneurial success.

Characteristics of Grit

To fulfill every goal that you set and find entrepreneurial success, you must possess the following essential characteristics of grit.

Bravery and Courage

Courage is a tough element to measure, but it is directly related to grit. The braver you are, the grittier you become. Being brave and courageous means that you can mitigate your fear of failing and aren't afraid to move forward despite the hardships that you experience. The super-gritty people aren't scared to tank. Instead, they embrace their fears as an inevitable part of the process.

People who possess grit understand that to accomplish their goals; they need to go through defeat and experience failure at some point in their life and they understand that they can learn valuable lessons from their past failures and mistakes. They know that the susceptibility of persistence is a pre-requisite for high accomplishment. Having the nerve to face your fears is a pre-requisite for being gritty.

Conscientiousness

Conscientiousness is the trait that is most closely linked with grit. There are two types of conscientious people: the achievement and goal-oriented ones and the self-controlling ones. If you are a goal and achievement-oriented individuals, you will stick with your mission until you accomplish all your goals. However, if you aren't achievement-oriented, you don't have the drive to move forward and achieve your goals. To have grit, you have to be conscientious to the extent that you chase your goals until you accomplish them.

Resilience

On the long journey to accomplishment and success, it is inevitable that you will stumble and fall. If you have grit, you will be able to pull yourself back up and eventually achieve the goals that you have set for yourself. This is known as resilience.

Resilience is described as the capacity to maintain and stick to your core purpose as well as maintain your integrity when you encounter surprises.

Resilience is a unique combination of confidence, creativity, and optimism. When combined these two qualities give you the power to reevaluate various situations and regulate your emotions. Your confidence in your abilities gives you the belief that you can influence your surroundings and the outcome of different events. Your creativity is what helps you to identify your meaningful purpose, and your optimism helps you understand that both the negative and positive experiences in life help you to continue to grow and learn.

Endurance and Setting Long-Term Goals

Another prominent characteristic that those who have grit possess is endurance. When you are following the path of successful entrepreneurs, you have to have the ability to endure all the roadblocks and challenges that you experience and stay committed to achieving your long-term goals. Along with having endurance and perseverance, being gritty requires you to set long-term goals and following them through.

To achieve success in life, you have to have long-term goals, and you must chase them to the very end. You have to be willing to invest long hours in your work and practice what you do best until you master it. This will allow you to eliminate all the obstacles in your path to achieve your goals eventually.

It is necessary that your practice has some purpose, or you will end up spending your time engaging in activities for no reason. When you don't have a purpose and aim in life, you can never become successful. To succeed at something, you have to have an ultimate goal that you want to reach. Your lifelong objectives provide you with the framework and context you need to find the value and meaning in your long-term efforts that help you to cultivate sustainability, drive, stamina, passion, courage, and grit.

Passion

When you are passionate about something, you become committed to achieving those things. Passion is another significant characteristic of grit. For you to become entirely dedicated to achieving your goals, you need to be passionate about them. This is because passion is what gives you the drive and compelling force to pursue even the most challenging tasks. Your passion is what motivates you to continue pursuing your goals. It keeps you going through the challenges and setbacks and keeps you devoted to accomplishing your goals even in worst-case scenarios. Being passionate about something is essential to becoming gritty.

Chapter 4 – Why You Need to Develop Grit to Become Successful

You just learned what it takes to be gritty, but do you know why it is vital to develop grit? Having grit is what will motivate you to pursue and achieve your dreams. Developing grit will help you to become motivated to train yourself to acquire this trait that will ensure your success.

It is Important for Survival

Many experts believe that grit is the top trait that you need if you want to survive anything. It is the quality that helps cadets survive West Point according to research. Grit enables you to become dedicated to one goal. It gives you the sense of direction you need and helps you to understand that the key to survive and thrive at anything is perseverance.

It Helps You Emerge Victoriously

Not only does grit help you overcome difficulties and survive setbacks, it ensures that you will eventually emerge victoriously. It is the one quality that differentiates those who win and those who lose. If you have grit, you know that nothing can stop you from winning. You may lose on occasion, but your dedication and mental toughness will keep you going day after day, and eventually, you will succeed despite the odds that are against you.

It Enables You to Pursue Your Dreams

When you have grit on your side, nothing remains impossible for you to accomplish because you know what it takes to overcome challenges and chase your dreams until they become a reality. If you have grit, you can set the most difficult goals and have the confidence that you will achieve them.

Grit Makes You Successful

One of the greatest things about grit is that it makes you prosperous and successful despite the fact that you may not be a super genius or amazingly talented. This is excellent news for everyone that might have a low IQ or who have been criticized by society for not having the talent to pursue their dreams. You don't need to have an exceedingly high IQ or superb intelligence to follow your passions and become successful. All you need it grit.

Grit Improves Your Self-Control

Your self-control or self-discipline is often considered the essential key to achieving your goals and staying dedicated to the path you're on. If you aren't disciplined enough to do what you need to do, then you will fail at accomplishing your goals. When you are disciplined, you are able to disregard and eliminate all the distractions that are keeping you from achieving your goals.

Furthermore, the self-control that you have, increases when you develop grit. This is because to acquire grit; you need to be strict with yourself and discipline yourself to the extent that you aren't getting distracted by the things that tend to shatter your focus. By working on building grit in yourself, you increase your self-discipline, which enhances your dedication to reaching your goals.

Grit Makes Your Fearless

When you have grit, you don't become scared of the obstacles that you face or any situation that you encounter. Your mind remains focused on the bigger picture that is never out of your sight. As a result, you see nothing but achieving your end goal, even when you face a frightening situation.

When you become fearless, you begin to gain the potential to overcome any obstacle you face in any situation. Grit gives you the power to beat the odds that are stacked against you and prove to the world that you can do anything.

It Unleashes Your Optimism, Confidence, and Creative Power

Another big reason why you need to develop your grit if you want to become a successful entrepreneur is that it helps you to unleash your optimism, confidence, and creative power. It gives you the ability to believe in yourself. This is important because it provides you with the ability to extract the positive out of the most negative and bleak situations that you face; helping you to develop a positive outlook on everything in your life. When you enhance your optimistic approach, your creative ability begins to grow. This gives you the ability to look outside the box and come up with new ideas to solve even the trickiest problems. Grit gives you the power to enhance your potential and accomplish anything you desire.

Grit is the essential trait that you need to develop if you want to become a successful entrepreneur. It brings with it many qualities that help to make you a better, more powerful, stronger individual that can accomplish everything they desire in life.

Chapter 5 – Habits of Gritty People

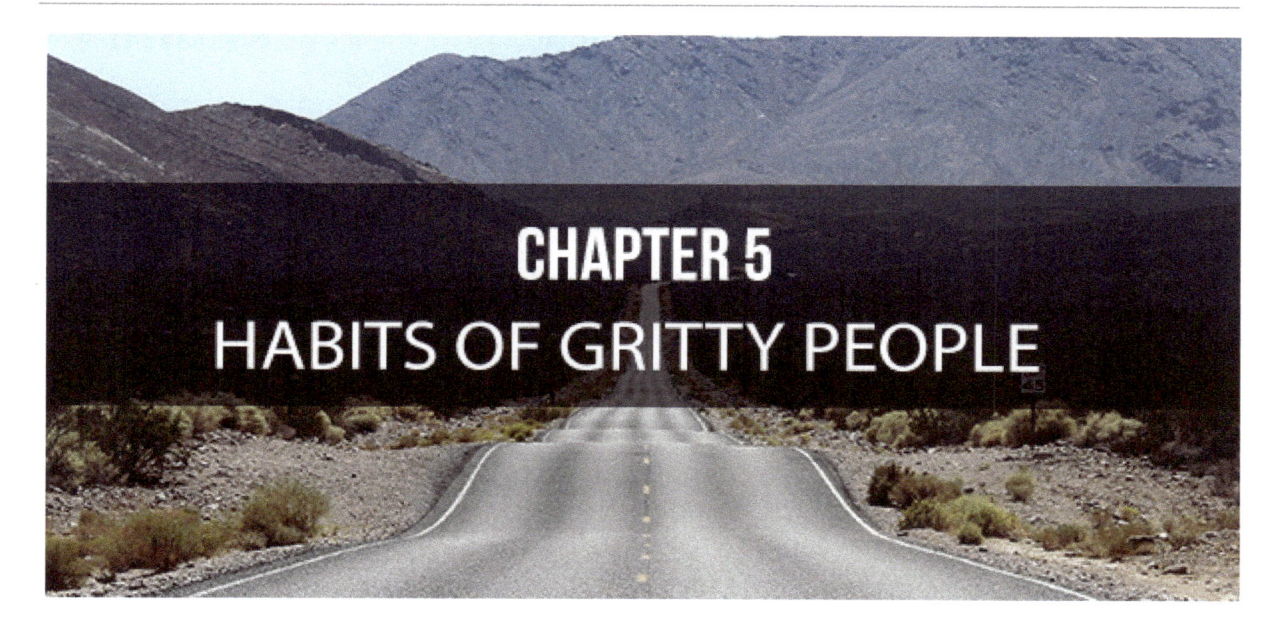

By now you should have a clear understanding of what grit is and why it is essential for you to develop if you want to find success as an entrepreneur. When you begin to understand the habits of gritty people, your understanding of what grit is should become more evident. Here are some things that all gritty people do that makes them successful in their entrepreneurial ventures. By learning these habits, you can start to work toward incorporating these practices into your journey to becoming gritty and finding success.

Always Show You're in Complete Control

A part of being gritty is acting as if everything is up to you and you alone. You need to show everyone that you are managing everything and are in complete control. This is what all gritty and successful people do.

Successful people don't concern themselves with the concepts of good and bad luck. Instead, they act as if their failures and successes are entirely in their control and they are the ones deciding whether they will fail or succeed, not a higher power. If they succeed or fail, they understand that it happened because of something they did or didn't do. They don't waste their mental energy on worrying about all the things that may or may not occur. Instead, they invest their efforts and hard work into making great things happen for them. They hold the belief that you have no control over luck or destiny, but you do have full control over yourself. They believe that you are the only person responsible for what you get in life.

To become gritty in your own life, you need to start to take control of yourself and everything in your life. You need to stop blaming your failures on bad luck and take back the reins of your life.

Learn Lessons from Your Past

Successful people never hold on to their past failures or mistakes. You will observe that while they have made several errors in their past, and have erred a million times, they don't hold on to it. Instead, they use their history as a means of valuable training and learn lessons from those mistakes, so they don't make the same mistakes in the future. When something horrible happens to them, or when they make a terrible mistake, they do get upset, but they don't dwell on it for too long.

Successful people with grit perceive their failures and past mistakes as a valuable opportunity to improve themselves and figure out what they did wrong. This is what helps them set and reach new milestones and discover better ways of finding success.

If you want to become successful and gritty, you have to stop dwelling on your past and the mistakes you've made. You have to realize that your past doesn't define you. In fact, your past is just a way of training and improving yourself. You need to think about what went wrong, figure out how to change your mistakes, and move forward.

Don't Stress Over Things You Can't Control

There is no point in wasting your time on things that you can't control. There will be times in your life that you won't have any control over what is happening. When this happens, you need to remember not to give them any importance and do what you plan to do anyway. If you want to gain the success you desire, you have to let go of the things you can't control. It's what all gritty people do.

Gritty people don't worry about the things that they can't change because they know it would be a waste of their time. Instead, they look at the situation and try to find a way to extract themselves from the mess, so even if things go wrong, they always have a plan B.

Never Criticize or Complain

If you don't already know this, your words possess complete power over you. When you say a negative thing about yourself, you instantly fall into the negativity trap and start thinking poorly about yourself. People with tremendous grit understand this, and it is why they never give their thoughts and words power over themselves. Instead, they empower their thoughts and manage them. When a problem arises, people with grit don't complain, criticize themselves or whine. They know that this will do them no good, making themselves feel weak instead. Alternatively, they take the matter seriously and assess it from an optimistic perspective, allowing them to find a solution from the problem.

If you want to be a successful entrepreneur and develop your grit, you need to do the same. You must learn never to waste your time and energy talking and thinking about what went wrong. Instead, you need to focus your energy on talking and thinking about ways you can make it better. This, in turn, will make you feel better, give you hope and eventually help you find a solution to the problem.

Be Conscious of Your Blessings

People who possess grit aren't just dedicated to their mission and aren't only working on strengthening their minds; they are also cognizant of all of the blessings that have been bestowed upon them and are conscious of them. They know how truly blessed they are and don't take any of it for granted. This is how they are able to improve their lives continually. They pay their gratitude to the universe. This helps them to find and invite better opportunities and experiences into their lives.

This is exactly what you will need to do if you want to become successful. You need to spend time every night thinking about everything you are blessed with and stop worrying about the things that you don't have. This will help you to feel better about yourself and encourage you to strive for even better things.

Celebrate the Success of Those Around You

Everyone becomes happy when they achieve success. However, to be genuinely gritty you need to celebrate the victories of your peers and competitors. This will help you to achieve the mental strength you need to be successful in your ventures. Genuinely gritty people don't frown when their competitors achieve success. Instead, they applaud their success and hard work. Praising successful people brings them closer to you, and when you surround yourself with successful people, you learn new and amazing things to help you improve your life.

Focus on Impressing Yourself

Trying to impress those around you is a waste of time and energy. Successful and gritty people understand this. They know that they will never be able to fully satisfy and impress everyone because of the knowledge that no matter what you do for other people, they will always complain about something. Instead, gritty people spend their time impressing themselves, allowing them to set higher goals for themselves. You need to focus on influencing and impressing yourself because you are the only one who truly cares and will always do what is in your best interest.

Be Specific

Successful people are specific about the goals that they set for themselves. When they embark on the journey to achieve their goals, they know exactly what they need to accomplish them. By being specific, they gain clarity and are able to remove any ambiguity regarding their goals. If you want to begin to achieve your objectives more successfully, you need to start being specific about what you want in your life.

Knowing exactly what you want to accomplish will help to keep you motivated in reaching your goals and help you keep moving forward until you've achieved them. Being specific allows you to devise a strategic plan for getting precisely what you want.

Act on Your Objective

Successful people tend to be extremely busy because they are trying to juggle several goals at once. Despite this, they still manage to complete all their work. This is possible because they seize the moment and act on their objectives as soon as they set them. When gritty people set a goal, they immediately start their journey for accomplishing them and take the first steps that are required to make them a reality. This is what sets them apart from the rest of the population.

If you want to enjoy the same success, you need to find a way to capture the moment and make the most of it by taking action toward achieving your goals. Stop wasting your time and do something beneficial.

Face Your Fears

Gritty people don't stop moving forward just because they've experienced a setback or ran into a challenge. They don't blame their failures on others. They face them with tenacity and courage and never stop moving forward. Facing their fears is what pushes them forward and eventually brings them success. If you want to develop your grit and become successful, you have to learn to embrace your fears with open arms.

Now that you know what habits you need to adopt to become gritty, you can move forward and start working to develop your own grit to become a successful entrepreneur.

Chapter 6 – How To Find Your Passion

MICHELLA
COSMETICS & SKINCARE

To start your journey to developing grit and succeeding as an entrepreneur, you need to find your passion and pursue it. This is the critical first step to having grit. You need to figure out what you are genuinely passionate about and go after it.

The things that you are genuinely passionate about and obsessive about involve adversity and challenges. You usually haven't mastered your passion, making them the things that drive you to improve yourself and inspire you to move forward with accomplishing your goals. Pursuing your passion is a gratifying process. This is why finding your passion is not only something that excites you but makes you do things you never thought you would.

When you set out to achieve your goals, you take an entirely new and different path than you're used to. This help you persevere, which is one of the characteristics of gritty people. An essential step in developing your grit is to discover what you are passionate about and start pursuing those passions. If you don't know what you are excited about, here are a few exercises you can practice to help you discover your passions.

Make a List of All the Things That You Love

Start by creating a list of everything that you love to do. Write down whatever comes into your mind. Keep jotting down ideas. This step is meant to help you focus on the things that you absolutely love to do.

Filter the List

Once you have completed writing down what you love, you need to filter it. Your list will contain many things that you love to do but aren't good at and things that you like the idea of but aren't interested in. Take the time to go through the list to find the things that truly excite you. Focus on each activity and find out the things that you enjoy and that you are good at. Taking the time to analyze your list will help you discover what you are genuinely passionate about.

Do the Activities

As you narrow down your list and discover the things that you believe you are passionate about, it is a good idea to carry out the shortlisted activities to find out if you are really passionate about them.

When you are doing the activities, you need to focus on the feeling you get. If it makes you feel good and excites you, it is something that you are passionate about. You get bonus points if it is something that you are good at too. Don't worry if you realize that you aren't good at some of the things that you are passionate about, you can become better with practice. Once you've discovered your true passion you can move onto the next step.

Take a Trip Down Memory Lane

Taking a trip down memory lane and revisiting your childhood is another way you can find your passion. As we grow older, we begin to disconnect from the things that meant the most to us during our childhood. To help you find your passion, revisit your childhood and think about the things that you loved to do back then. You may find your passion during your visit.

Seek Out People You Want to Imitate

There will be people in your life who inspire you to follow your goals. There will also be those people in your life who have achieved the kind of success you've always dreamed about. To find your passion, figure out how they did it and what made them focused and determined enough to reach their dreams. This exercise will help you become passionate and focused on your goals. It also gives you the change to figure out that one role model you want to follow. Identifying a role model will help you figure out what you are passionate about.

Develop a Creativity Board

Browse through magazines and websites and gather the images, newspaper clippings, poems, articles, and other material that is related to the things you enjoy and that inspire you. Place these elements on a big poster board, being sure to have separate columns for each interest. Begin to build on each interest and think of creative ideas to create a business out of your interests.

You will be brimming with ideas for those interests that you are passionate about. Don't stop until you have figured out a master plan to create a career out of that interest.

Don't Focus on Money

To find what you are truly passionate about, you have to stop focusing on money. You need to focus on that one thing that makes you feel alive. If you want to enjoy a quality life, then you need to do something that you love, whether it is something that will make you money or not. Your financial concerns should be a secondary thought to your passion.

Chapter 7 – Face Your Fears

You can never develop your grit if you aren't able to welcome and embrace your fears with open arms. If you are dedicated to your mission of becoming gritty, you have to accept this. Facing and battling your fears is the only way you can move forward and develop grit.

Even the more successful people in the world didn't achieve their goals quickly. They had to face a lot of challenges on their journey to success, but their willpower and determination helped them continue to move forward. They were able to meet their fears head on because they all possessed the grit they needed to follow their passions and achieve the goals they set.

Get Comfortable with Fear

The first step that you need to take is to become comfortable with the fact that fears and challenges do exist. When you reject them and the desire you have to move forward without encountering them, you become scared of them the moment you experience them. However, when you make peace with the fact that fears and challenges are an inevitable part of the entrepreneurial journey, you will begin to understand that when you face them, you will start to reduce your anxiety.

To help you get comfortable with the idea of fear, you need to tell yourself that "Fears are a part of life and it's okay if I come across obstacles on my way to success. I will fight and end them and emerge victoriously." When you tell yourself this about 20 times within a couple of minutes, your fear will automatically begin to diminish.

You also need to write down all your fears so that you can validate them. This exercise helps you to understand that there will be obstacles that you will have to face down on your journey to entrepreneurial success.

Make Your Positive Thoughts Your Dominate Thoughts

Nurturing positive thoughts is believed to help you attract success, prosperity, and abundance. This is what is known as the law of attraction. The best way to keep fear at bay is to make your positive thoughts dominant over your negative ones. This can be done with daily affirmations.

Affirmations are the positive suggestions that you feed your mind to make it believe that you will only experience good things and that you are achieving your goals. By creating positive affirmations, you are causing your mind generate positive thoughts. These positive feelings begin to take over the negative ones, bringing exciting things into your life.

To practice affirmations, you need to create a positive suggestion based on your goal or fear and repeat it daily. It is vital that you keep your suggestions center on the present. For instance, rather than saying, "I'm, going to become successful," you would want your affirmation to say, "I am successful." Here are some positive affirmations that you can begin to use in your life.

- I am incredibly successful because I always think positively.
- I find it easy to face my fears and overcome them to emerge victoriously.
- My optimism gives me the strength to overcome challenges and find success.

Start Small

Fear comes in many different shapes and sizes. Not every fear that you will face will be too big or grand. Even the tiniest of fears have enough power to break you into a million pieces. An excellent way to fight your fears is to start small and keep moving forward. Just like you break larger tasks into several smaller ones to make the task easier to manage, you need to take small steps to face your fears. Starting small helps you reduce your fear and forces you to take action rather than cursing your fears.

Keep Practicing

As the saying goes, practice makes perfect. When you begin fighting your fears, you will have instances where they return. Each time your fear returns, the obstacles appear to grow bigger, eventually forcing you to stop fighting your fears. However, once you stop fighting your fears, you show them that you don't dare to continue to fight, leaving them to overpower you. If you want to overcome the challenges and confront your fears, you need to keep practicing.

The first time you lose, you need to take a step back and analyze the entire scenario to determine what went wrong. Then you need to try again, using the new strategies you've devised. You will fail several times in your quest, but your practice and perseverance will eventually end the battle, allowing you to emerge successfully. Perseverance is an essential trait that you need to develop in yourself if you want to become successful.

Don't Dwell on Scarcity

People who quit when things begin to get tough tend to dwell on scarcity. This is because they cannot achieve anything significant. This results in them accepting what little they have and prevents them from trying harder. While being happy with what you have is great because it makes you content, you should never dwell on scarcity.

Starting off with these steps will help you make progress toward reaching your goals. Self-appreciation will encourage you to face your challenges with a more significant force.

Chapter 8 – Build Your Perseverance

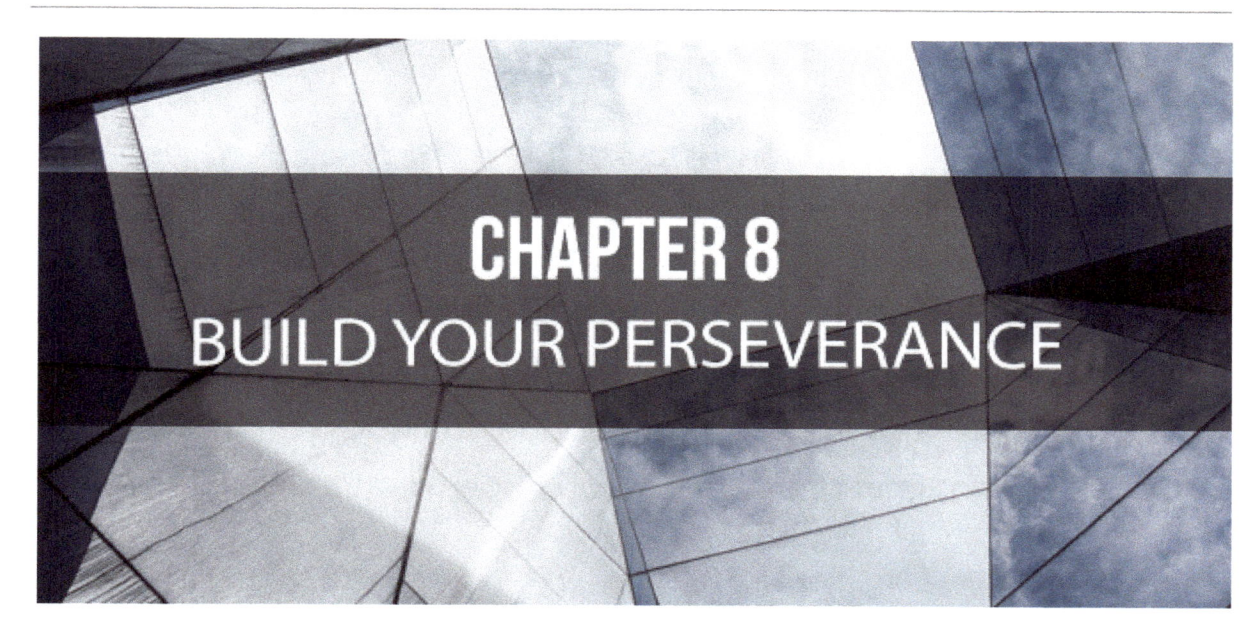

Perseverance is defined as the ability to stick to your goals and pursue them even in the midst of challenges and setbacks. You lose all of your assets, you become physically ill, and you encounter a million other obstacles on your journey toward success, but you continue to move forward toward your goal. You continue to move toward your goal, even after losing everything, you push on and finally accomplish your goals. This is precisely what having perseverance makes you do and this is a trait that all gritty people have in common. They persevere and never take the back seat when they are forced to face a challenge. This is exactly why they succeed, and if you want to succeed in your journey, you will need to build perseverance as well.

Here are the things that you can do to learn about persistence and to build your endurance.

Know Your Goal

The first step to developing your perseverance is to know exactly what you want to achieve. You need to identify what you want so that you know what you need to work toward until the very end. Since you have already been taught how to find your passion and your lifelong goals in chapter six, you know what to do.

Remove Any Self-Doubt You May Have

On your journey to achieving success, you will encounter numerous hurdles and challenges. One of the most frightening and debilitating obstacles you will have to overcome will be your self-doubt. There may come a time as you work toward accomplishing your goals when you will begin to doubt your abilities and will lose your confidence, making it difficult for you to continue to move forward. This is why it is important for you to figure out how to remove self-doubt from the equation and replace it with persistence.

Make a list of all of your strengths and focus on those for a time. Tell yourself positive things about yourself and tell yourself that your strengths are enough to take you forward.

Along with focusing on your strengths, you need to prepare affirmations around your self-doubt and tell yourself that you have faith in your abilities. Repeat those statements several times a day, and within a couple of weeks, you will find that your self-doubt has been reduced.

Keep track of your progress by recording the steps that you take on your journey. This will help you to track your performance and allow you to become conscious of your accomplishments. When you make a note of your smaller achievements, you become stimulated and stop doubting yourself.

Keep Your Emotions in Check

On your journey to entrepreneurial success, you will encounter many stressful events. You may even get hung up on them. Doing this will only drain you of the energy that you could be using to do something more productive. A critical component of preserving is to perfect your ability to keep your emotions in check and let go of stresses. Maintaining your calm during stressful moments can help you save your valuable energy to be used later doing something better. This can be easier said than done, but you always want to try.

To stay cool, you need to take some time to think before you speak or act. When something upsetting happens, learn to walk away from the situation and take several deep breaths. Refrain from speaking or acting on a thought until you have thoroughly thought about the issue. Take five to six deep breaths and inhale through your nose, exhaling through your mouth. You will begin to feel your stomach distend as you breathe in and out. Soon you will notice that your anger has already started to subside, giving you the clarity to realize that you were upset over nothing. Once you can calm the storm inside, you can think clearly and rationally, helping you to save valuable time and energy.

Know Your Core Values

The most appropriate way for you to move forward in any situation is by having a firm grasp on your core values. Knowing your core values will also keep you focused on moving forward to reach your goals. Your core beliefs are the values that you stand for and the principles that you follow in your daily life.

To figure out what your core values are, you need to read about different kinds of perspectives and figure out what concepts, issues, ideas, and beliefs you feel strongly about. When you find something that actively moves you, you should spend some time meditating on it to know what your conscience says about it.

To meditate on something, you need to find a peaceful spot to sit and think on the subject that influenced you. Take a few deep breaths before you begin pondering on it. This helps to relax your mind and slows down your thoughts, allowing you to focus on a single topic. As you start to relax, you'll want to start to ruminate on the issue and let your thoughts flow freely. Find out what your mind has to say about the issue and pay attention to how you feel about it. This practice helps you to form the core values that you will always stand for. This will gradually shape your perseverance.

Keep Pushing Forward

Once you've gone through the previous steps, you need to continue to push yourself forward. You already understand that obstacles and setbacks are a part of the journey, and you know what you need to execute and move closer to your goals. Now is the time to give yourself a big push forward and keep moving toward your goals.

There will be days during your journey when you don't have the motivation to complete the steps necessary to move closer to your goal. In those times, you need to stick with it and persist. When you experience a setback, take some time to calm yourself and regroup; quickly getting back on track and pushing yourself forward. Don't give yourself a lot of time to relax because when you remain stagnant for too long, you will begin to lose motivation and interest in your goal.

When you experience disappointment, tell yourself that it's not the end of the world. Instead of thinking there is no way out, remember why your plan took an unexpected turn. Tell yourself that there is hope and ignite the positivity spark that is in you and you won't end up giving into your fears.

How to Deal with Unexpected Issues

A vital part of staying persistent and building perseverance is to deal with the unexpected challenges and obstacles that you experience in the right way. You need to deal with the hindrances and glitches you encounter rationally, so you can learn from your mistakes. Here are some ways to deal with unexpected issues.

Face the Harsh Reality

You need to stare the harsh realities and challenges that you experience in life right in the face. It is not something that is easy to do, but by doing this, you are given an edge over everyone else. This will help you to manage yourself through each issue. Rather than ignoring a problem, you need to see it for what is, so you can find out how to best deal with it. You need to be truthful and honest with yourself in this regard. You also need to stop playing the blame game. You have the power over yourself, and if you haven't been doing anything right, it is your fault, so the only person you can blame is yourself. Finally, you need to stop putting things off until tomorrow if you know that you can do something today. Deal with any issues that arise, as they arise.

Carefully Weigh the Options

When an issue arises, you need to make a caution, logical, and rational decision on how to deal with the problem rather than making a rash decision and regretting it later. Weighing your options carefully will help you come up with a strategic plan to move forward with your goals.

As important as it is to analyze the situation on your own, it is also wise to get an opinion from someone who is experienced on the subject. Consult with them and consider their suggestions. Then take some time to weigh the pros and cons. Go over the problem a final time and create several plans that can counter it. After you have developed multiple solutions, assess each one individually, then opt for the most logical solution.

Listen to Your Inner Voice

Your inner voice or conscience should be your final deciding factor. After you've analyzed the entire unexpected issue, you need to listen to your inner voice to see what it has to say. Sit somewhere quiet and focus on the whole situation, then close your eyes and think about the problem. You will begin to hear some voices, or maybe even see some images. This is your conscience providing you with a message. Take the time to ponder what it is saying so you can comprehend the message. This will help you to take the right step forward.

Once you've completed these steps, you need to stand up for yourself and stand your ground on the decision you've made. You may very well have made the wrong choice, but it is important not to back down and to learn from the mistake. This is how successful people gain insight and forge ahead on their path.

For you to move forward on your path to entrepreneurial success, you need to master how to be resilient in everything you want to accomplish.

Chapter 9 - Become More Resilient and Boost Your Stubbornness

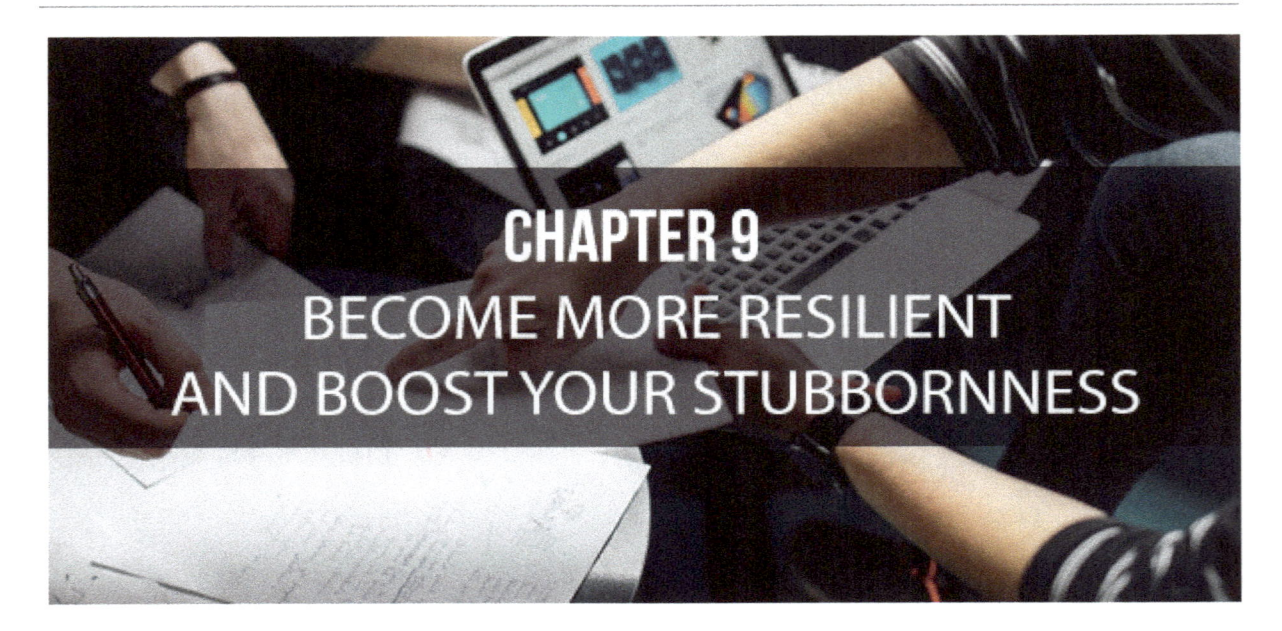

As you start on your journey to perseverance, you need to work on your resilience as well as your stubbornness. These two qualities are essential for you to develop and strengthen your grit. To establish the hardiness you need to succeed in business you need to complete the following steps.

Keep Your Mind and Body Healthy

A cloudy mind and out of shape body prevents you from being able to get past the hurdles that are in your way. This is why it is so vital for you to properly nourish your body and your mind and work at keeping them healthy. You need to take daily measures to ensure that both your body and mind are in a healthy state so that you can stay healthy and tough in the most challenging times.

To do this, you need to make sure that you are eating sensible and nutritious meals. You need to add lean cuts of meat, whole grains, dairy, seeds and nuts, essential oils, and fresh fruits and vegetables to your diet. It is imperative that you avoid eating foods that contain artificial and processed ingredients, trans-fat, and genetically modified organisms. You should increase your daily water intake, so you can better regulate your metabolism and other processes that take place inside your body. Doing all of this will keep you healthy and active.

You need to make sure you remain active, getting at least 30 minutes of exercise a day. This can be anything from yoga, swimming, running, aerobics, or anything that gets your heart pumping. Regular exercise helps you improve your stamina, strength, and brainpower. It is also essential to get enough sleep every day. Shoot for seven to eight hours of sleep a night, with a 30 to 60-minute nap during the day.

Keep Everything in Perspective

For you to remain focused on your goal, it is vital for you to keep things in perspective. To do this, you'll want to keep a log of all the activities you perform and their outcome. You also must learn to live in the present, so you don't become distracted by what has already happened or what may happen in the future. When you lose your perspective, you run the risk of getting lost in the negativity trap and worry incessantly for no reason. This is why it is so important to live in the moment and remain focused on what you currently have.

To truly live in the moment, you must be dedicated to practicing positive self-talk and keeping your mind focused on everything that you currently have. You also need to become fully involved in the different activities you currently participate in, so you don't lose your focus. To gain better insight into an issue that you may be facing, try looking at it from someone else's perspective. Put yourself in the shoes of others and try to feel their emotions as you work through the issue.

Nurture Your Spirituality

A good way for you to hone the sense that you are a part of something bigger is to nourish your spirituality. Being connected with your spirituality helps you to identify your purpose when you lose sight of it. To help you nurture your spirituality you to need to meditate as often as possible.

To gain the full benefits of meditation, you need to find a quiet space where you can sit comfortably and breath naturally. Focus on your breathing. When you feel your thoughts, start to stray, and you become distracted, bring your mind back to your breathing. Spend 10 minutes a day doing this until you can successfully concentrate on your breathing through the entire session. When you can concentrate on your breathing for the entire session successfully, you can begin to prolong your meditation. This will help you to gain a better insight into how your mind works, and it will allow you to tap into your spiritual side.

To build your resilience and develop your grit you have to stay true to your goal and practice these steps on a regular basis. In addition to this, you have to be stubborn.

Why Stubbornness is an Important Part of Grit

When you hear the word stubborn, what you do you think? If you're like most people, you instantly picture someone who has bad manners and an ill temper. Stubbornness has gotten a bad reputation, and is often associated with negative traits like defensive, self-centered, overly competitive, and controlling. While many of these characteristics are held by people that are stubborn, being stubborn isn't an entirely bad thing, especially when it comes to grit.

According to Angela Duckworth's study stubbornness is a crucial characteristic of grit. It gives you the power to move forward with your goals and ideas.

It Helps You Know What You Desire

Not being easily impressed with every other opinion that comes your way doesn't mean that you are self-centered and stubborn. It merely says that you know exactly what you want. Gritty people are stubborn because it helps them understand precisely what they want and don't want in their life.

When you are clear about your goals, you can make the right decision and pursue your goals without becoming distracted. Gritty people have an amazing focus thanks to their stubbornness. This is why it is a good thing to be stubborn if you want to develop your grit.

It Makes You Persevere at All Times

When others flounder during a storm, you can keep your head held high, because of your stubbornness. It helps you understand that challenges and setbacks are inevitable and that at some point they will pass, allowing you to persevere instead of crumbling. Stubbornness is the reason why gritty and successful people can fulfill every goal they set.

It Makes You Stand by Your Values

Being stubborn means that you are aware of your core principles and that you will stand by them no matter what. It means that you won't follow the crowds and do something that you don't want to do. Stubbornness is what makes successful people stay true to their values and stick with what they believe matters most.

It makes you defy the odds.

Chapter 10 – Boost Your Confidence, Optimism, and Creativity

Confidence, optimism, and creativity are three of the most prominent elements of grit. Your confidence is what makes you believe in yourself and boosts your self-esteem. Your optimism helps you to think positively even during the worst of times. Your creativity allows you to look outside the box for solutions to your problems and enables you to deal with tricky situations. The following sections will show you how you can begin to develop these qualities, making it easier to build your grit.

Tips for Boosting Your Self-Confidence

Here are some proven tips that will help you to boost your self-confidence easily.

Practice Positive Affirmations

The best way to develop your self-confidence is to practice positive affirmations daily. You just need to build a positive suggestion that helps to assure you that you are confident. Say it loudly, over and over again. Find a place that is quiet and peaceful to limit distractions. Here are a few confidence affirmations that can help you get started.

- With each breath, I exhale stress and inhale confidence.
- I succeed at everything I do because I am incredibly confident and sure of myself.
- With each passing moment, my confidence multiplies.
- It is effortless to feel confident and relaxed.
- I have complete confidence in myself and my abilities.

You will begin to recognize a remarkable improvement in your self-esteem when you practice these suggestions at least 20 minutes a day for two weeks. If you aren't able to practice them for 20 minutes at a time, once a day, you can always break it down into two 10 minutes sessions twice a day, or even 5-minute sessions four times a day. The critical thing to remember is that you need to practice every day to realize the benefits.

Practice High Power Postures

Harvard School of Business professor, Amy Cudy has discovered during her research that there are specific body postures, known as the high-power body postures, that will boost your testosterone levels and reduce cortisol levels. Cortisol and testosterone are hormones that your body produces and are linked to making you stressful and improving your confidence respectively. Your confidence level begins to improve when these changes take place within your body. Cudy has also shown that high power body language is one of the reasons why successful people are gritty and able to accomplish their goals more efficiently because their cortisol levels are exceedingly low compared to the levels of testosterone. To help your confidence reach amazingly high levels, you should incorporate high power body language into your daily life.

Always be Prepared

One way to boost your confidence is to be prepared for the things you plan to do. Many times, we lose our confidence because we fear we don't know everything about a subject and are scared that something might come up that will shake our confidence. To fight this fear, always try to prepare yourself for all the tasks that you participate in.

Keep Track of Your Accomplishments

Keeping a record of what you do will help you keep track of all that you accomplish. This allows you to look at them from time to time and feel a sense of pride. This also encourages you and helps you to understand that you have what it takes to accomplish everything you set out to do.

Dress the Part

Dressing sharply plays a significant role in developing and increasing your self-esteem. This is because when you look good, you feel good. When you feel good, your confidence rises. Also, when you play the part and look sharp, people will think that you have full command over the subject and listen to you attentively.

Speak Clearly and Slowly

People tend to quickly lose interest in a topic when you rush through your presentation. When you talk clearly and slowly, you will more than likely garner more attention because people will be able to understand what you are talking about. Speaking clearly and slowly also helps them feel that you know what you're saying and have complete command of the topic. As soon as you notice that people are taking notice of what you are saying, you see an immediate boost in your confidence.

Tips for Boosting Your Positive Thinking

To get yourself out of messy and adverse situations, you need to develop positive thinking. Here are some compelling strategies to give your optimistic approach a boost, so you always think optimistically and continue to build your grit.

Meditate Regularly

Regular meditation can help you become more positive over time. Meditation also enables you to build valuable skills and qualities that tend to stay with you for a long time; this includes grit. When you meditate regularly, you begin to display increased concentration, mindfulness, and positivity. Follow the guidelines shared with you earlier in this book and start to make meditation a daily part of your life.

Write About Your Positive Experiences

Writing about your positive experiences can lead to you having better and positive mood levels and fewer illnesses. To develop and strengthen your grit, you should make a habit of writing down your positive experiences every day and think about them for about 10 minutes. This will help to stimulate the production of positive, healthy thoughts, leading to an improvement in your state of well-being.

Do Things You Enjoy

Schedule time throughout your week to do things that you love to do. This can help to calm your mind and boost the serotonin levels in your body. Serotonin is a hormone linked to improving your mood. When you increase your serotonin levels, you become happier and think being to think more positively about your life and the world around you.

Incorporate these strategies into your life to help you unlock your inner confidence and positive thinking.

Tips for Tapping into Your Creative Side

Here are some easy strategies for developing your creativity and boosting your innovative skills.

Re-Conceptualize the Issue

Creative individuals have the habit of re-conceptualizing a problem before they begin doing an innovative task or come up with an imaginative creation. In order to do this, you need to look at an issue from a different perspective. Try asking your support system how they perceive a situation and then try thinking about it from their perspective. This can help you to tackle any situation from different angles and come up with creative solutions.

Jot Down Ideas

As you begin to brainstorm ideas, it's a good idea to make notes in a journal, anything that comes to your mind, even if it's a single word. Ideas tend to disappear as soon as they pop into your brain, putting them down on paper makes them concrete.

Exercise Counterfactual Thinking

Counteractive thinking is best known as the "what if" theory which states that if you question yourself the possibility of different things relating to a problem or idea, you can come up with inventive solutions while enhancing your creativity. To practice this theory in your daily life, you need to ask yourself, "What else can I do?" or "What may have been?" When you ask yourself these types of questions, your mind starts looking for answers to them. This is because our brains have been designed to accept questions and look for their answers. When your mind is in active thinking mode, you begin to brainstorm and analyze issues from a different perspective. This helps to boost your innovative power and helps you to become more creative.

To tap into your creative side and harness the power of creativity, carry out these exercises and increase your grit.

Conclusion

The people who achieve the most success in their lives are not those who have found a way to avoid making mistakes or encountering obstacles. The most successful people know that mistakes and challenges are an unavoidable part of life and they are the ones who are willing to keep moving forward after making mistakes and experiencing failure. These people have what is known as grit.

Your grit is what matters most for whether or not you will succeed or fail at your entrepreneurial venture. You've now been shown the way for developing your grit and harnessing its incredible power to become a successful entrepreneur. You've learned what it takes to become a grittier person and overcome life's ongoing challenges. Following this advice will help you become grittier, allowing you to enjoy more success and accomplish everything you set out to do.

Knowing the traits that every entrepreneur possesses and how you can nurture your entrepreneurial spirit can help you on the path to developing your grit and along your journey to becoming a successful entrepreneur. Take these lessons to heart and come back to them often as you may your way through the process and face challenges and setbacks on your entrepreneurial journey. Anyone can become an entrepreneur, but only the grittiest ones are able to find lifelong success.

CPSIA information can be obtained
at www.ICGtesting.com
Printed in the USA
BVHW012025210123
656720BV00002B/67

9 781034 518174